The Song Castle

The Song Castle

Michael Kiesow Moore

NODIN PRESS

Cover art: Nora Moore
Design and layout: John Toren

978-1-947237-24-7

Library of Congress Control Number: 2019947955

Nodin Press, LLC
5114 Cedar Lake Road
Minneapolis, MN
55416

www.nodinpress.com

for Mom

Contents

NOT A ONE ORDINARY

SIGNS OF THE TIMES

THE LIBERATED SPACE

THE SILVER SKIFF

THE SONG CASTLE

I want to build a song sturdy as a castle
with rooms – it must have rooms!
A room that can hold Lorca's full moon rising,
a room for Whitman's calamus leaves, fecund and green,
a room vast enough to hold the rage of Achilles
and another to hold the fall of Troy –
and we can give Wilfred Owen that room for it will
be large enough to hold, too, the pity of war.
Once we fill all these rooms, can we finally
find room enough for love?
First we must find the lost key
dropped so many times it is a wonder it
has any form at all, or held so fast by
some it can only be removed by the
white nimble fingers of Death.
Let us then make prodigious rooms for love
and hand out the keys prolifically
to all who deserve one and more so
to the ones who do not – for is this not
a love song, like all the songs?
And when we finish building this great
edifice it will beat in the deep heart
of this cold cold world and the song will
suffuse every living being
and you will be held
all manner of living beings will be held
and no one will ever be alone again.

Two Men Holding Hands

Tonight two men walked on the sidewalk
holding hands. It was a summer evening.

We were going the same direction for a bit.
I watched one man lean down and

kiss his boyfriend lightly on the cheek.
They smiled, lost in their world of two.

Seeing these men, hand in hand,
brought to mind the last time I walked thus,

holding hands with a boyfriend, a summery
day along Lake of the Isles. We

were just walking, enjoying being together.
A young woman skated by on rollerblades

and screamed "Faggot!" She said more.
I think we were going to Hell because we

held hands. I hate that memory.
As I watch these two men I send

them a hope, that as they walk
this evening hand in hand the

people they encounter smile at them,
maybe even give a high five. No, let

me take that back. Not even that. What
I wish for them is that nothing happens,

that tonight and every time they walk
it is as ordinary as breathing.

Death Comes Knocking at My Door

When I saw Death standing at my doorstep
I thought of the speech I long prepared.
"Why did you take them away, why so many?
Did you have to take Keith and Bill and Frederic
and Mahlon and Tim and Hunter and Kerry –
I could go on with the names all day."
Sometimes when I compose this long rehearsed
speech, I also ask, "Why them and not me?"
All these words hung in the air unspoken
as I watched how tired Death looked.
Death's bones bowed with weariness.
"So, do you want to come in?" I asked.
Death gave no answer but walked in
and sat in my living room chair.
I dropped over the tired bones my favorite
afghan quilt knitted by my grandma.
I almost said, you are now wrapped by the
love of one more you stole, but held my tongue.
I made Death a cup of tea, who took it
gratefully. And we sat. In silence.
The strangeness of Death sitting in
my living room, covered by my grandma's
wool afghan, sipping tea wore off.
We were not strangers to each other.
Then Death stood, handed me the tea cup,
the afghan dropping to the chair.
As Death crossed my threshold I said,
"I suppose I will see you again one day."

A LIFE LIVED IN BOOKS

It is a life lived in books – begins in books,
then soaked in books and will surely end in books.
Blame my parents, a bookshelf our first furniture.
Never enough shelves. The books took over—flinging
themselves on tabletops, chairs, the floor.
Nobody dared cook without one.
No joke: my first toys were books. I built forts
of leather-bound bricks of Tolstoy and Sophocles.
Look close when you visit, or a stray will
send you flying to an early death in books.

The Night Owls

for Lars Krogstad Ortiz

If we Night Owls were in charge, no one would get up before 9 am. What will get the stares is anyone up at the crack of dawn.

Eight hour workdays won't be needed, punch clocks either. Once we get to work, we are an industrious bunch. Even if we start late in the day, breaks are still required. Long ones.

The big social hour is dinner time. Plan on mealtimes that start at 8:00 pm and run into the night. Some may return to work after dinner when they know they will be most productive.

Things begin to wind down after midnight. There will be some who will want to be social for a while yet, others who want personal time.

For artists this time will be sacred. What joy to attend to your craft when you feel most alive and not worry about an alarm clock going off just when you're ready to go to sleep!

If we Night Owls were in charge, we would throw nighttime festivals, stringing everything we could get our hands on with lights—festivals of light sparkling through the night.

Paintings would fill with celebrations of the moon in all its phases, the starlit sky, the glittering dream that is the Milky Way. Some artists could paint a sunrise just to be different.

When summer solstice arrives, we would welcome the coming longer nights. The long days were lovely, but we so look forward to the deepening nights again.

Songs and poems would sing of our favorite totem animals: bats, opossums, and owls. Ecstatic cats worldwide would leap for joy that humans were finally on *their* schedule.

When we use the language of Night whenever we speak of Death (because we love the Night so much) Death itself is never feared when it comes.

If Night Owls were in charge, people would discover that you do not live to work, but you work to live. People would love life more. Stress would fade away. Except maybe for the Early Birds.

RAISING THE BEATLES FLAG

Friends tell me stories of how they came to the Beatles. Many tales tell of the famous broadcast on the Ed Sullivan show. One friend growing up in a household that watched Lawrence Welk defied her parents that night. Even though it meant getting no dinner, she watched that famous broadcast on the family's basement TV. There were saltine crackers in the basement. She reports that her dinner of crackers that night was "worth it."

I do not have such stories. I was too young for the famous night. To me, the Beatles became *that* group my frenzied female babysitters screamed about. Over time school kids brought in their newly purchased 45 LPs to show off, displaying that green apple that was cut in half on one side.

I was slow to rock and roll. My favorite "B" bands started out with Beethoven and Bach, even at that young age. Yet there was something I noticed. If I claimed allegiance to that rock group who had songs like "Let it Be" blazoned on the latest 45, I was spared getting beat up that day. For a few brief moments I could appear like everyone else, and they forgot how different I was from them. Raising my hand to the flag of the Beatles protected me, sometimes.

Looking at My Younger Self with Walt Whitman

In his late years, what did Walt Whitman think of his younger self, who at age 37 first sang his Song of Myself? Did he wish he was that young again? Did he think the younger self naïve? If he could go back in time would he change anything? Would he love differently? When the Civil War broke the country, would he still expend his every once of energy helping the dying souls, even though attending to the needs of the dying men just about killed him? Give me more men to love was his daily answer.

We get hints of these answers in his preface to the final edition of *Leaves of Grass*. No apologies, no regrets. In his final years he lauded the open sexuality of his verse, particularly the Calamus poems celebrating "manly love," writing that "the espousing principle of those lines gives breath of life to my whole scheme that the bulk of the pieces might as well have been left unwritten were those lines omitted." Bravo, Walt.

I spent this afternoon looking back at my younger self. Knowing what I do now about the costs of AIDS on my life, what it took from me and the ways I still suffer, would I make the same choices? Would I still sit with the dying man, this stranger—me—when no family member would, helping him pass through the veil knowing he was not alone? Would I still make the dinners, clean the homes; would I wipe every bum, sterilize every needle, wash soaked bed sheets, bathe the stick men? (Mind you—like Walt—my training was as a poet not a nurse.) What could I change? Give me more hands to hold. Give me more bums to wipe. Give me more men to love.

GANYMEDE WITH THE EAGLE

marble sculpture by Bertel Thorvaldsen,
Minneapolis Institute of Art

The naked youth leans to the great
eagle, Zeus now made beak and
claw, and offers the raptorgod a drink.
The sculpture is a contrast between sharp
and smooth, deathmaker and lifegiver.
For this moment the Thunderer stands
subdued, feathered head leaning to the
lad, enraptured by smooth-skin manly
innocence, submitting.
Zeus will be the prisoner, desire
more binding than iron.

Too Long a Man

I have been a man so long I forgot what I was.

I ask the ash trees dropping sad yellow leaves.
That is no answer!
I ask a squirrel soon to be seized by an owl.
That is no answer!
I ask the Mississippi River rushing to the indifferent sea.
That is no answer!
I stare in a mirror to see who stands behind the stranger's skin.
That is no answer!
I rearrange my bones and they curse my question.
That is no answer!

I have been a man so long I forgot what I was.

ALL OUR SOULS ARE FILLED WITH IT

And time – how strangely does it go its ways –
First we are heedless – Lo! 'tis as nothing!
Then a sudden waking, and we feel naught else but it.
All the world tells of it, all our souls are filled with it …
    – from Der Rosenkavalier, *Richard Strauss and Hugo von*
    Hoffmansthal

Do you see Time when you look at me?
How it spills from my pores,
and rushes out my mouth.

I almost remember when it was
a tiny little trickle. I cupped my hands,
took small sips. It was sweet then.

When did this torrential cascade burst?
My body cannot hold the pounding waves.
Stand back lest you be swept away, too.

THE NIGHT SLAYER

On the day of the longest night they gathered,
they lit candles, and by hearth fires
told stories of dire monsters and how heroes
vanquished them.

We gather as well today, and do we not
have our own monsters to slay?
Do we not want the feelings of fear and dread
to disperse?

Where is the Beowulf for our own times,
someone to slay our Grendel
so that we can finally welcome the coming sun
with songs of joy?

Tonight the dark feels heavy. It feels like it
will always be night. I reach for a feeling
of hope for the future, but it slips my grasp.
Tell me a story.

THE POET WHO LOVES THE WORLD

for Lynette Reini-Grandell

Last night I heard a friend
give a poetry reading.
Her every poem was
suffused with her holy
love for the world.
There was no distance
between her heart
and everything.
Is my heart open,
or did it close?
Do I still love
the world?

REALITY WEARS US SO THIN

Reality wears us so thin, a poet
said. When in profile, do I
completely vanish? I look in
the mirror and see my ten-
year-old self. He admonishes
me. I gaze out the window
and watch cars pass by and
hear sirens. Where are the old
trees? The living room turns into
ice. We are all translucent here.

DEPRESSION

sun and moon exchange places
impersonal daylight touches cold skin

words fall out of books by multitudes
withering like worms on pale ground

salted rain slowly drips from
blackened leaves of bonewhite trees

something heaves below ocean waves
not even the whales speak its name

middle C goes flat on all instruments
musicians lose hope and find new careers

Yes is bound by rusty chains
lost in chambers forgotten

at night, the scorching
desires burst into hateful things

dreams grow heavy and sweat
as color seeps out of the days

someone stands on a high bridge
is it you? me? another lost soul?

the river slows beneath, waiting
the air itself holds its breath

THE FIRST RAIN

Wash over
us rain, break
apart crusts
of ice and
salt, crack
open our
minds so
memories
pour out
until all
is blank
again,
sunder our
shells and
make us
naked to
the new day.
Innocent
again we
grasp hands,
washed.

Lorca, the Moonlight, and Me

Would that Federico García Lorca walked beside me tonight.
The full moon shines so bright that the light casts day-like shadows.
It almost hurts the eyes to stare at the sunlighted moon.
I picture Federico standing beside me, arms lifting to the moon,
an Andalusian song rising from the depths of his belly.
Then—Federico's lips touching my ear—he whispers,
"I will remember this night as long as I live."

NÄCKEN

All these years I thought I was immune.
That would never happen to me.
I walk through the woods and a wood nymph jumps out.
"Honey," I say. "Please put something on."
At the stream, a water sprite emerges, revealing her breasts.
"Girlfriend, you're not my type."
Over time I hear the stories. The men overcome by desire,
dragged to cursed realms. Sometimes a woman succumbs, too.
I am not the only gay one walking these woods.
And then it happened.
One day I hear a man's voice, humming a tune
so lovely the trees themselves bow to listen.
I glance down at the river. An inhumanly beautiful man
lounges on some rocks, naked. He stands and steps into the water,
calling me to join him, his silvery arms outstretched.
Then by some magic a violin appears in his open hands,
and he begins to play. The manly beauty of his body is enough.
Desire fills my soul and until there is nothing left of me but Want.
And his music. Why does he have to play so divinely?
Do they tell a story of a man who walked
into the woods and fell in love with a beautiful Näcken—
and then was never seen again?
I hope when they finish telling this story,
the man ensnared says he has no regrets.

THE SILVER SKIFF

Under the oaks we veer in a silver skiff.
                              —Georg Trakl

It is such a small boat that skims above infinity.
Do you ever look over the rim
to gaze at the depths we glide over
or do you keep your eyes locked on the body
of our little boat, telling yourself,
this is the whole world,
the oar is a city that will never die,
at the prow my true love, a bronze statue who
will stand thousands of years, golden and perfect,
each passenger here a heroic poem who will be
sung and remembered for as long
as we know how to sing the old songs?
Have you noticed the waters below quicken?
Did you look to see where we race to?
The multitude of stars above blink out
one by one. Is it dawn's blush or
were we wrong about everything?

LOST AND FOUND

To Wake from a Dream

for Deborah Keenan

is like a fish leaping into the air.
Suddenly two worlds visible at once.

How can this be? This awareness is a shock.
The world below was perfectly real, with all its

rainbow-colored reefs, schools of angel fish,
pulsating green seaweeds and purple anemones,

and the monsters, always monsters.
And then there is this, something sitting

above the known world. It looms. Strange
sounds and deep rumbles. A veil covers this world.

And yet it calls, more insistent than the Sirens' song
that tortured Odysseus. The fish wants to go back

to the ocean depths but is powerless, is flying,
flying faster to that other, bizarre realm.

And the ordinary proclaims its weight.
And the fish, landed, out of flight

landing, the fish is no fish anymore.
And that apprehension the greatest shock.

The Year Gentleness Died

It was the year gentleness died.
Larry was first to go
the sweet young man covered with purple lesions.
He was the sweetest. Men can be sweet, you know.

Then it was Keith's turn.
He was a rebel rouser, full of righteous anger.
But at his core he was all gentleness.
And it was a plague against the gentle.

And then Frederic went,
dear lovely Frederic.
His spirt was like a puppy's
bouncing and joyful, always joyful,
and now gone.

I could tell you about Bill
and his love of angels because he was one,
and if you never met Kerry—
I could do this all day, telling you
all whom we lost the year gentleness died.

They went in the tens, then the hundreds,
we lost them by the thousands,
then ten times that across all the lands.
They kept falling, all the gentle ones.

Do You Remember When Words Had Power?

With the right Word you could turn into a wolf or a bear or a hummingbird.

With another Word, a skunk or a snake could turn into a human.

In those days distinctions were not made.

Do you remember when the Word could make a dream real, or the other way around?

Do you remember when you shared your True Name only with your beloved because of the magic you gave away?

Are those Words still out there waiting to be spoken again?

THE TRACE OF US

Walking on
a nature
trail today
the asphalt
buckled,
tree roots
pushed
up
and
plants of
every kind
filled cracks
and
crevices.
Soon there
will be
no trail.
Just woods.
Strange
to take
comfort
in watching
nature
remove
all
trace
of us.

A WOLF DREAMS HE IS ME

It is a strange dream, being inside the skin of a man. It feels like I sit on my haunches watching from inside, seeing the things unfold through his eyes. I go through his day, first sipping a morning coffee—black, then putting clothes on, driving in a car. I know what cars are from the outside. But if I just sit and watch, I can observe my manself do the driving. And then this man spends his day typing at a computer. What a horror of a dream! All these things keep this man from tearing his clothes off and running through the woods. Does he never dream of leaping at a deer and tearing its throat, the blood gushing into his mouth? What is this thing called "tofu", and why does he use implements to eat? The day ends with this man taking a bath, sitting in hot water, drinking tea. I like being naked again, and the water is strangely soothing. This is not awful. But the worst part of this dream is smelling nothing. It is as if the world in all its rich dimensions go flat and lose its color. I never get used to that. Finally the dream ends and I awake to cold air brushing my fur. I take a whiff. I smell the world.

The Beautiful Energy of the Bullpen

for Norton Stillman

a bricolage from: "Bullpen wilts in eighth inning" (Star Tribune, September 10, 2017) and "The Beautiful Energy of Thoughts" (Shambhala Sun, May 2012)

free us from a tangled web
of entrenched habits

hot hands loosen the grip of
the vicious cycle of misery

real source of the problem:
nobody on base

a curve into the left field
corner traps us in a perpetual

cycle of the revolving-door
of an illusory sinker

pure energy arising from emptiness
knows how to grind it out

breaking balls
transcend ordinary

the cause of our suffering
wilts the bullpen

bases loaded in the second inning
rest in this vast space

late innings leave no trace
above the fray

WORTHY APPEALS

a bricolage from: Minnesota Public Radio appeals letter,
September 26, 2017 and "Be Free Now: an interview with Jack
Kornfield", Lion's Roar, July 2017

you receive many worthy appeals
to live in joy
join with us
no matter where you are
make the switch today
to quiet the mind
increase your commitment
step-by-step
bring your tears
the body will leave
outside of time
the great mystery
be unwavering
we can all do this
live in love
discover what's beautiful
we are incredibly grateful

I Dreamed That I Broke Into Robert Bly's House

Last night I dreamed that I broke into Robert Bly's house.
A friend convinced me that we should steal his books
and sell them. Robert Bly was not home and we cased his
bookshelves. I was disappointed. I already had many of the
books myself. Then we looked at his shelves of LP records.
I put one on a phonograph player. A lovely piano quintet.
Could have been Schubert. The LP cover was a photograph
of the musicians, men in black suits and skinny ties. We never
got around to stealing his books. So Mr. Bly if you ever
hear about this, I apologize for dreaming that I broke into
your house. I won't take your books. Some of your words,
though, is another story.

Church Basement Percolator Coffee

dedicated to Erik Skogen

a found poem, "North Shore," Minnesota Monthly, September 2017

bone-chilling currents of
church basement percolator coffee
pushed a junked car
into the pool—
tossed and submerged—
into a rocky gorge:
the pinnacle of coffee geekdom

COSMIC MOLTEN CHOCOLATE SOUFFLÉ

a bricolage of words and phrases from Molten Chocolate Soufflé
www.chefsteps.com and Target Earth: The Next Extinction from
Space (Discover Magazine, September 9, 2016)

Add death star, invisible substance, and comet—
combine with hands until they form together,
leaving no dark matter. Add controlling gravity,
whisk until dissolved. Cook on low heat until
mixture has a thick, gummy texture.
Add chocolate. Note, reaction could
heat Earth's core. Won't be pretty.

STAR PEOPLE

We forget who
we are, that
our very
molecules are
made from stars.
Would we not
treat each other
more kindly if
every day we
greeted each
other with the
words, "Hello
fellow child
of the stars.
I see the shine
of the stars
in your eyes.
Will you see
the light of
the stars in
mine?"

DREAM GIFTS

Last night I dreamed that it was Christmas and everyone
gave to each other gifts of what each person cherished most.
My brother gave me the first poster of KISS he ever bought,
Gene Simmons in all his leather-clad glory. I gave my brother
in return the first album I bought, an LP recording of Verdi's
La Traviata, with Beverly Sills on the cover wearing a lacy,
white party gown. My brother does not like opera nor have a
turntable, but he cherished this gift because it was something
I dearly loved. And so it went. Aprons and expensive shoes
were exchanged for fishing lures and worn tee-shirts.
Everyone accepted each gift with abundant joy.

NOT A ONE ORDINARY

ORDINARY CREATURES

I look for the ordinary creatures:
the black beetle running by my feet,
the white sulfur butterfly fluttering by,
the honeybee wresting pollen from a
drooping yellow goldenrod,
a common gray moth lifting from grass,
mosquitos touching my arm,
a squirrel gathering one more acorn,
a couple turkeys ambling by the woods,
the grasshopper suddenly taking flight.
All these creatures want to live.
Not a one ordinary.

Before the May Day Dances

for Jason Ritenour, 2017

Before the May Day dances
began we gathered to hear
the announcement: you
were in a car crash and died
this morning. And then the
show went on. Why this
imperative, to keep going?
Let it all come to a halt.
The trees wish to weep with us,
and the owl in the woods has a
lament to sing. Would that the
earth ceases its rotation, if only
for a little while, and time itself
stop its relentless roll.

The snow falls now as I write
this poem, and muffles the
wail of nearby sirens.
Earlier today some of us
visited the spot where you died,
and danced. We danced for you
and all who are taken suddenly.
We danced remembering
the light of your glittery smile.
The circles of our bodies
held your memory, and then we
stopped, our hands high in the air.

APRIL SNOW

for Carol Connolly

Facebook today was flooded with photos of April snow: trees
laden with white globs, decks covered in white, streetlamplit
snow flying down like swift meteors. Those who did not
post photos posted curses. I did not take a picture, but there
is snow covering my little porch, and the city sidewalks are
likewise white laden. For a brief moment, I look to this
night's snowfall as a chance to accept things as they are. Just
the other night, I heard a favorite octogenarian poet at a
reading say with a loud and firm voice, "We are lucky to be
here."

KIN

I name you kin
osprey flying above
and you loons leaping
below the water surface
and the water of this lake,
you are kin
and trees—all of them—
and this one tree,
the one right here
in front of me,
friendly white pine who
greets me year after year,
who I look at from the
window each day,
you are my kin.

THE TREES PACK THEIR BAGS

"American trees are moving west and no one knows why", The Atlantic, *May 17, 2017*

Honey, you can't bring that rock with you. I know you got used to how it nestled under your roots, but we need to travel light. They have rocks out west. You might even find one that you like better. And how many times have I told you why we're moving? We heard that life is better out West. More sunlight, more rain. The soil is very rich. You'll love it. Take my word, okay? And don't worry about the fires. Your dad has a map and we are not going anywhere near them. We will be safe where we're going. And they say there are no politicians there. Enough said?

Nothing At All

for Kathryn Kysar

It began like a madcap comedy.
I waited outside at a coffee shop,
sitting on a cold metal bench
where I could watch the Mississippi River
plied with traffic of barges and river boats.
You were running late and texted me:
if I ride towards you, we could meet on the path,
that mystical place where the lost and the late
always find each other.
It was a lovely idea,
but we were riding different bike paths.

So you texted me to stay put and you would find me.
I watched the Mississippi quietly flow,
trees in the distance turning red, yellow, and bronze.
You pedaled up the hill, breathless.
I pointed out where you could see the wake of
the spring floods on the tall trees across from us,
the jumbled tangles of tree roots suddenly made visible
like troops of aged naked men who thought they would
never show themselves to the world this way again,
tangles of bleached arms and legs like skeleton bones,
vulnerable as babies.

We ride into the woods along old paths of broken asphalt,
the bikes jiggle and clang as
acorns and twigs crunch under our tires.
Then like curtains revealing the long awaited stage,

44

the river materializes again.
It is right there, at the same level as our bikes,
flowing as tender as an Orphean song,
as if it was nothing at all,
as if it was as ordinary as words on paper.

IF I WAS HUMAN NO MORE

for Jim Moore

Let me be a river.
Not for the way no part of a river is the same.
Not for the go-with-the-flowness of rivers.
Not for how there is no such thing as a straight line—
the way rivers move North to South but not pencil straight.
All these could be good reasons to be a river.
What I want is the long view.
How long have the Mississippi or the Amazon or the Nile been flowing?
They see things by the thousands of years.
If someone builds a dam, the river will acquiesce for a while.
Will the dam be there in a thousand years? Ten thousand?
If such a marvel occurred, the river could change course and go around,
or over time finally wear the cement back to limestone grains again.
What would our own lives be like if we had such a view?

Everything would matter.

SHIMMER

for Morgan Grayce Willow

The ancient Greeks believed
the gods did not permit mortals
to see them, that to do so would
be so overwhelming it would lead
to death, which is what happens
when Semele is granted her desire
to see Zeus with her own eyes.

What we mortals are permitted
to see is a shimmer, a glimmer.
The Greek language is full of
words expressing the divine shine.

From a distance today I saw a
cloud of gold maples leaves
sparkle in the fall sunlight,
gilt light dancing pirouettes.
For a brief moment it seemed
I watched Aphrodite glide by,
the hem of her glistening robe
catching late afternoon godlight.

THE VIOLETS

for John Medeiros

"The violets in the mountains have broken the rocks."
– Tennessee Williams, Camino Real

You know the names they call us. I will not repeat them.
They think we are weak. They know we do not like to fight
back. But we are not weak. And we are not cowards. Watch
as our roots dig deep into the hardest stone, the rocks that
they cannot break even with the chisels of their sharpened
tongues. It will not happen over night. We are the patient
ones. But it will happen. A day will come and the rocks will
break apart. We violets can tumble mountains.

KEITH

for Keith Gann (1958-1990)

I am from you, Keith,
the nights we danced together—
how we loved the dance.
And I am from your ferocity
for social justice. Being in
ACT UP was another kind of dance.
Do the people of Mora, Minnesota
still talk of the busload of us activists
showing up in that small town?
They probably never saw so many
placards again after that day.
I think of that March on Washington
and how you and Perry sat with
my mom watching the NAMES Project
quilt unfurl over the silent Mall.
Do they still talk about how, after
walking the long route, and how
passing the White House we yelled
"Shame!" so loud it seemed the
white edifice would join the walls of Jericho,
how after all the tears, and gazing
at the quilt panels memorializing
our fallen, how after the speeches
and applauding and crying out
for justice, how as the sun set,
music played from someone's radio,
we danced? Lord how we danced.

I Am

Nov. 22, 2016—An eight-point doe was shot in Abrams in northeastern Wisconsin. The doe likely had a higher testosterone level, something that might occur in one of 100,000 deer. The deer, which had female genitalia, was tagged a buck because the antlers were at least three inches long.

Were you surprised when antlers pushed through skin?
How did male deer treat you, did they want to fight?

Did you want to lock antlers with the males?
Did you hold more power looking like one of them?

Or did nothing change at all, your partner entirely happy
to mate with one who looks like himself?

Does being female and male both feel as normal as saying, I am?

GLUING LEAVES BACK ON TREES

I spent the day gluing leaves back onto the trees.
I began with the maples, big red ones.
Then turned to the brown oak leavings.
Many who walked by shook their heads, what
a lunatic there, trying to hold fast to autumn.
A couple children joined me in the task, they
needed no explaining, they knew what to do.
Most old people would have nothing to do with this.
But one ol' gal wearing jeans jumped in,
of all of the crew she glued with the most zeal,
as if each leaf was a year of her life.
At the day's end we admired our work.
Leaves were glued tight, and winter must wait.

THE DAY-JOB MOTH

*Although moths are typically nocturnal, winter moths have
adapted to fly during the day in frigid temperatures, sipping
the witch hazel's nectar and spreading its pollen.*

— from Chris Hardman's Ecological Calendar

The Day-Job Moth shows up at the first witch
hazel—late—and gets a tongue lashing. Not
my fault! It's freezing first thing in the
morning! It takes a while for my wings to
work. And then some stupid bird tried to
eat me for its breakfast. You should
be glad I make it here at all.

The Day-Job Moth moves on to the next
witch hazel. Not a word. The cold shoulder.
You should be thankful I do this at all!
If I didn't visit all you flowers every day,
your pollen would not get spread.
You should be more grateful.
Without me your kind would die out.

At noon the Day-Job Moth takes a
rest. The Order of Day-Job Moth
United established rules that allow for
a half hour for lunch and two fifteen-
minute breaks in the course of the
work day. Time goes all too quickly
and the Day-Job Moth flies off.

It is a long, cold day and the sun
sets earlier and earlier. Before the
Day-Job Moth knows it, it is time to call
it a day and he flutters off to home.
The Day-Job Moth does not know how
much longer he can do this work.
But what else can he do?

LEARNING A DEAD LANGUAGE

for my guide through ancient Greek, Ryan Seaberg

You pore over the grammar charts.
The old words feel like marbles in your mouth.
You can spend the rest of your life studying this
dead language and no one knows for sure
if you are pronouncing the words right.

You will never have a conversation in this language,
never order a coffee or ask where the restroom.
But if pressed, you can make a statement about how
you will be grievous to enemies and loving to friends,
how this makes for a glorious life.

You hope, with all this study—
oh that wicked grammar—something of
these ancient people still has wings.
Truly there is a glory in speaking aloud
the winged words fleeing the pull of the grave.

WINTER'S NIGHT SPEAKS

I welcome Winter's Night like an old friend,
the deep silences that wrap about me
like a dear quilt. Tonight I was still enough
to hear it speak, "slow, slow, slow" it said.
How strange we must seem to Winter's Night,
no sense like the many other animals who
sleep the cold winter season away.
We, instead, scurry as if it was still summer.
"slow, slow, slow" — do you hear?

ODE TO KAREN'S PULLA

for Karen Lassila

Sing praise to the
grandmothers, who
kneading flour, yeast,
milk, egg, and butter,
pressing the dough
with palms, folding
it again and again,
forming balls, all
through the years,
expressed their love
with every push of
hands, filling warm
kitchens with smells
of yeasty dough.

And let us sing praise
to the Vikings—yes,
Vikings! For on
their travels they
learned of the
jewel of spices:
sweet cardamom,
grown tenderly in
India, and escorted
to Constantinople,
where all roads
converged. Did the
Vikings know what

they brought back
would blossom
in the cuisine of all
Scandinavia?
Who first thought
it a good idea?
One person's whim,
can shape a culture.
Let us sing then to
that Viking – woman or
man – who first
sniffed the spice,
and then said to the
merchant, More.

Let us praise
Karen's forebears,
and her own mom
who yearly baked
the Finnish bread,
keeping alive
the splendid
traditions reaching
down the centuries.

And let us take a
moment to praise
all the ways coffee
made its way to

the Northern lands—
more nods to
Turkey—for no
other beverage
tastes better with
warm, buttered Pulla.

And let us praise
Karen herself, who
at Yuletide, year
after year, kneads
the gifts of Vikings
and grandmothers,
in her own kitchen,
braiding nine loaves
as gifts, filling her
hearth with the
scent of yeast
and cardamom.

Another word for
Pulla is love.

SIGNS OF THE TIMES

THE WAR, 1919

painting by George Mayer-Marton,
Minneapolis Institute of Art

The drawing shows a
crowd of refugees, backs
bowed, many carrying
bulging rucksacks over
shoulders, one man
perhaps carrying a
child in his arms. They
cross a desolate plain, a
bare-limbed tree in the
foreground. The figures
are small. At first glance
you only see a horde,
lost below masses of
black clouds that press
down upon them. One
man stands out with his
arms thrown into the air.
This work of art is nearly
one hundred years old.
It could be today.

Manning Up in the 21st Century

1: Metamorphosis

When I was a boy they said I crossed my legs like a girl. Then they said I held my books like a girl. I try to remember how I once moved my loose wrists, the tender ways I walked through the world. I must have been soft once, if only because of the taunts hurled at me that still haunt. It did not happen over night. I stopped crossing my legs and holding my books like a girl. My wrists hardened. The rest of me froze, too. Sometimes I try to be like I once was. Hard work after turning me into stone.

2: Displays of Masculinity at the Saint Paul Farmers Market

At the Farmers Market today I saw a blond-haired manly man who stood at the vegetable stand, legs in wide stance like the Colossus of Rhodes, feet planted, and body taut as if saying, "Don't even think of picking up this last bag of basil." He stood beside his girlfriend, and likewise his not-an-ounce-of-body fat toned body yelled, "MY girlfriend! Mine!" It was a wimpy bunch of basil he wanted so I moved on. At a nearby stand I found what I spent the last half hour jostling through thick forests of elbows and immobile baby strollers for: piles of fresh basil, picked this morning, fragrant, the air blossoming with basil fragrance. The young man tending the stall—probably for his mom—was just as sweet. After I made my purchase, I stopped to consult my shopping list. Then that manly man and HIS girlfriend stopped and looked at my bag on the ground, blooming with rich, green basil. "Where did you get that basil?" the manly man asked. I pointed to the nearby stall. He shook his head and said, "Your basil is better than mine." I was not competing and I won.

3: Waiting for the Door to Open

You stand in front of the door to the women's restroom. And pause. You just stand there. Wondering. What will it be this time? Usually it is not what is said. It is "the look." They try to hide what they are thinking, but they cannot hide the moment of surprise, the sudden flash of fear. You look at the door to the men's restroom. You spent your life until now walking through that door, and each time it felt like a lie. You are done with that lie. But they say you should keep using that room. And what kind of looks would you get dressed in your best dress and red pumps? They do not want you there either. And here you are again. Standing. Waiting for the door to open.

ATHENA SHAKES HER HEAD

There is a moment in Homer's *Iliad* that chills me to the bone:
The people of Troy—the women and elders not fighting—
parade to the Temple of Athena, led by Queen Hecuba
who herself selected the most valuable robe in her stores
to give to the goddess. At the temple the High Priestess
lays the gorgeous, scarlet robe on the statue's knees,
and promises to make sacrifice right there,
a cow unblemished and never touched by a prod.
The voices cry out as the priestess implores the
goddess to take pity on the people of Troy,
on the women, the old people, and the children.
The great head of Athena, the god even more
warrior than Ares, the protector of the city,
shakes her head — no. This is the only time in
the thousands of lines poem that a god communicates
directly to mere mortals. And the answer is No.
The people will perish.
And those who do not die will be made
slaves and concubines to the conquerors.
What a thing to hear from a god.

How many times have such supplications
in the four thousand years since the making
of this poem been given such an answer?
How many times has this answer been made
in our own lifetime?
I think of the Syrian people of Aleppo,
surrounded by enemies, bombs falling
through the night. What prayers
did they make? How many prayed to

America as if we have replaced Athena,
the god of the new age who the suffering
offer petitions for salvation?
In America the people cry over a photo
of a little, wounded boy in an ambulance.
We weep.
Write a poem or two.
We shake our collective head.

How to Explain How Things Are Today

We must have forgotten
something along the way.
Did we misplace a key,
or maybe it was a
photograph, the most
important one? Maybe
it was a word we
stopped saying over
time. Or how we looked
at each other, *that* way.
Did we not once ask
what Silence had to say?
It must be something
irrevocably important
that we all forgot.

My Cloak

I put Hope on today, a tattered cloak
held together with so many rainbow-hued
patches you cannot tell its original color.

Children laugh at me as I walk by.
You should hear the adults.

One day an old man walks up to me.
He says he once had a cloak just like mine.
He lost it and cannot find it again.

I used to make speeches, explain why I wear it.
I do not do that anymore.
I tire of explaining why everyone should wear such a garment.
Besides, I do not wear Hope for them.

Childe Rowland, the Killer of Elves

#1

Playing ball with her brothers,
Burd Ellen chases a ball
widdershins around a church,
and thereby is lost to the
world of Elfland.

Her brothers go on a quest
to retrieve her, and the first
two never return.

Rowland, the youngest,
then learns what
he must do to save them:
in the land of Elfland
he must neither
eat nor drink, and
he has to kill
everyone he meets.

Elves are evil, so what
does it matter if any die?

#2

As Rowland wanders
Elfland, elves keep
offering him food
and drink. "You look

thirsty," says a
cowherd. "Are you
hungry?" asks a
henwife.

Rowland kills them all.
They are elves.
Who will miss them?

#3

Rowland dispatches
each elf he meets,
including a kind horseherd,
who, like everyone he
meets, keeps offering
to slake his hunger
and thirst.

When the elves ask why
he slaughters them so,
Rowland answers,
"I am only doing
what I was told to do.
I am not a bad person."

#4

Most tellings of this
tale end happily,

Rowland subduing
the Elf King, and
freeing his siblings.

Praise the hero, the
killer of evil elves.

WORLD AIDS DAY

They say that the birds of song will return.
Can you still hear in those vaulted cathedrals

the sweet trills that, for most of us, are
but the faintest of echoes now?

Have the silences reigned so long that
should the great flocks return in all their

resplendent glory—the peacock green,
bunting indigo, tanager scarlet—we

would say to them, not so loud
please, you are too bright.

The gray skies are so quiet.

MURDER OF BLACK CROWS

Tonight I witness black crows wing
to the sky, hundreds flying above
my head, then settling in

denuded branches of empty trees,
now full of black canopies, the crows
hammering relentless, strident cries.

Are these bleak yells angry?
It is not my fault, I want to answer.
"The lands drown! The lands burn!"

I watch the dying crepuscular sky
darken with black wings as the
voices keep shouting prophecy.

THE SIGNS OF THE TIMES

The Signs of the Times #1
The ancient Greeks saw signs
everywhere: the meaning of birds
flying above—especially the
flight of an eagle—the
entrails of sacrificed animals;
there were even specialists,
dream interpreters and
soothsayers known as bird seers.
Stars give signs, too,
bright Kuna—the Dog Star—
harken evil times.

The Signs of the Times #2
The bird seer gazes at the entrails,
deformed and corrupted;
the dream interpreters are told
images of shooting guns,
the lands exploding with bombs —
the stars themselves turning
the color of blood.
Here is one true story:
on December 12, 2016
vandals broke into a LGBTI
Southeast Asian community center
in Rhode Island, and hung a noose
from the rafters.

Signs of the Times #3
Pro bono lawyers.
They storm the airport.

As many as two hundred fifty
lawyers are signed up,
giving help and advice
to the Muslim
travelers, green card
and visa holders,
who the current
regime tries to ban
from our shores.
The lawyers stand in
airport lobbies declaiming
we are a nation of laws.

Signs of the Times #4
A Jewish university
student entered his
dorm room and found
on a whiteboard a
drawing of a swastika
and concentration camp.
In big letters, "Nazis rule."

In a Facebook post,
the student asked,
"What benefit do you
gain by making a
person feel afraid?"

Signs of the Times #5
A Hmong family who lives
in the suburbs of Minneapolis,
woke to find and evil word

painted in huge letters on
their garage door. The two
parents, two brothers and sister
found their car vandalized, too.

When word got out in the
neighborhood, a neighbor
helped remove the graffiti.

Signs of the Times #6
Minnesota's largest library system,
the Hennepin County Library,
posted in all 41 libraries the sign,
"All are welcome here."
Said a librarian, "We're one
of the cornerstones of democracy."

Sign of the Times #7
There was another
bomb threat
today at a local
Jewish Community
Center. Everyone
was rushed out,
mostly elderly and
pre-schoolers.
What memories
lurched from the
shadows for the elders?
What lessons did
the young children
learn today?

Signs of the Times #8
After the White House withdrew
protections for transgender students
in schools, a 13-year old transgender
boy tells his mom he does not
want to go to school anymore.

Signs of the Times #9
In a suburb of Kansas City,
a white man harassed two
men from India, assuming
they were Middle Eastern,
yelling "get out of my
country." He shot the two
men, and Srinivas Kuchibhotla
died of his injuries. Another
man who tried to calm
the situation, a peacemaker,
was shot and wounded.

Signs of the Times #10
Outside the Minneapolis Institute of Arts,
people gathered with signs like
"Una clase, una lucha — contra fronteras
[one class, one struggle — against borders]!"
and "Don't deport our fellow workers."

Neo-Nazis showed up, entered the
museum. Some protestors entered, too.
On the third floor, amid furniture
of the 18th century, fisticuffs ensued.
No arrests made, a knife confiscated.

There are few places in the city I
consider more of a haven than this
museum, walls hung with paintings
by Rembrandt, van Gogh, and Soutine.
I go there to remember who I am.

Fist fights and neo-Nazis in the MIA.
I do not recognize my precious world.

Signs of the Times #11
"Muslims offer to guard Jewish graves"

After bomb threats to Jewish
community centers and vandalism
at two Jewish cemeteries,
many Muslims said on Twitter that
they will stand guard at Jewish JCCs,
synagogues, and cemeteries.
Said one on Twitter:
"I'm a #MuslimMarine in Chicagoland
area. If your synagogue or Jewish
cemetery needs someone to stand
guard, count me in. Islam requires it."

Signs of the Times #12
Another black man
shot by a white
policeman in
[*write latest city name here*]

Signs of the Times #13
His name was Richard Collins III.
About to graduate from Bowie State University, Maryland.
He was commissioned as a second lieutenant in the Army.
And he was black.
May 20, 2017 he waited for an Uber ride at a bus stop.
A man approached and said:
"Step left, step left if you know what's best for you."
Collins said no and the man—Sean Urbanski—
plunged a knife into his chest. Collins died.
The killer is a member of a group called Alt-Reich Nation.
Many who tell this story call it a lynching.

Signs of the Times #14
"The political moral is
certainly depressing:
these people could be made
to believe anybody or anything."
From *The Berlin Stories* by
Christopher Isherwood,
published in 1945.

Signs of the Times #15
Statistics you will not see on TV tonight:

In 2017, there were 29 deaths of transgender people
in the United States due to fatal violence,
the most ever recorded.

American Indian women face murder rates that
are more than 10 times the national average.

It is said that there is still no reliable way of knowing
how many Native women go missing each year.

The Signs of the Times #16

An El Salvadoran
man and his
daughter,
seeking asylum,
wash up on
the shores of
America
dead,
the toddler
still clinging
to her dad.
Hearing the
news, the
Statue of
Liberty
lowers her
once ever-
burning
torch.

Signs of the Times #17
"Valedictorian dares to disturb the universe"
Ozaukee Press, June 25, 2018

The setting was the town where my family lives in Wisconsin, at the school where my niece and nephew have attended, Port Washington High School. The newspaper headline quotes a line from a T.S. Eliot poem that the school Valedictorian, Violet Huegerich, used in her speech on June 3, 2018, at my nephew's high school graduation ceremony. She urged her classmates to take risks, to strive for success, to contribute to society, and most importantly, be themselves. "...[D]are to disturb the universe and change something for the better." Then Huegerich next told her classmates: "Time is the most precious thing we have, and with it we can do all these things and more. For instance, time gives me the chance to come out as a woman who happens to be transgender in front of my entire graduating class. If you didn't catch it earlier, my name is Vi. Have I disturbed anyone's universe yet?" Until that moment Violet was Tommy Huegerich. My sister-in-law, Lisa, who heard her speech, said the announcement was greeted with raucous applause. Violet then sat down in her place in the "H" row and remained seated until the Principal called her name —"Violet Huegerich"— and she shook hands, received her diploma, and walked off the stage into the future her words and deeds fashioned.

THE LOST LANGUAGE

I dream of finding a lost language,
a language that has no words for war
or any kind of violence a human can
make against another.
This old, forgotten language
will be wise in the use of gender,
not binary.
This language won't even have the
word for binary.
And this will be a language that has more
words for love than the colors of
a large box of crayons,
each word a new shade of care,
and so vast that dictionaries fill
to the brim with every different hue.
And all the colors of the human clan
will be described by those words of love,
for when you speak of your fellow
beings with love,
how could you ever harm one?
If we cannot find this long, lost language,
then let us make it now.

THE LIBERATED SPACE

The Liberated Space

*"To read a Surrealist poem is to survey a territorial tract—
however modest in size—of liberated space."*
        —from The Poetry of Surrealism: An Anthology,
        edited by Michael Benedikt

Have you seen the Liberated Space and yes that space
holds barracudas who swim with can openers and Cocoa
Puffs along with crazed men pointing guns but they will
be wearing pink tutus and dance in sparkly red high heels
and the stars will sprinkle the cubicles of our jobs with
showers of silver glitter and who wants beige anyway or the
incessant thought patterns that grow ruts and bar you from
uncovering your true self and who cares what anyone thinks
anyway because the Moon, the Moon who sees all our secrets
sings the Ballade of Federico Garcia Lorca and the song sinks
deep into the earth where gravebound bones shed the dusty
tears and the lands tremble oh how they tremble while snow-
white horses meet at the lost grave and poets across the lands
take pickaxes and shovels in hand to dig for their wildhearts
revealing with every new word and even the crossed out
ones the long lost Liberated Space that will be their and
everyone's salvation

Do Not Reject the World

Why is it so easy
to say, no not
this? I want it
different. Not
what I asked for.

Can I cup my hands
to the runnels of
regret, let the
sharp shards
sit in my palm?

I want to say, this
is how it is, tell
my reflection, you
are fine. We are
all good here.

Six of Swords

The boat has six swords plunged into its frame.
There is one driven even into its floor.
The boat should leak, but it does not.
The oarsman asks where I want to go.

"What does it matter? All destinations
end up the same whenever we do this.
Take me where you will. It all looks alike."
We head out once more. At least

it is a familiar journey, even if
I want to be anywhere but on this boat.
All of a sudden a purple finch lands
on the boat's rim and sings. The little

bird sings as if it was born to make
only this one song. I feel like I hear
music for the very first time.
I did not expect that to happen.

When Mom Read to Me

Can I remember my mom reading to me as a child?
I know she read to me often.
Mom and dad both love books.
I remember going to the library
my brother and I,
returning home with armloads of books.
Library Day was the best day.
Mom surely read to me.
I remember going to used bookstores.
There was one in Ellicott City.
Floor to ceiling books, new adventures
within every slightly musty binding.
One day, leaving the store,
Mom looked in her billfold and said,
"Oh no, I just spent the grocery money."
No doubt Mom read to me.
Why can't I remember?
Was I so eager to read the stories myself,
that I jumped from my mother's
lap as soon as I could?
I have the dimmest memory, a huge book,
on the cover a painting of a magic white
bear carrying a girl on its back, mom's
favorite book when she was a girl,
brimming with stories of witches,
giants, and curses. And happy endings.
If I still my thoughts, I can almost hear
Mom's voice, "Once upon a time…."

ARIADNE'S LINE

It is a long line this thread, the ancient Greek word for thread—linon—the source for all our threads, linen, and "line" itself, a line of poetry, a fishing line, a line of music, draw a line. Ariadne gave Theseus two implements to survive the labyrinth of Minos—a sword to kill the Minotaur (in Greek, "Minotauro" or "Minos' bull") and the famous thread, that cord, leading the way back through the maze, back to safety and life. Grab hold of any kind of line, a finish line, a timeline, a line of duty, the A line, a line of latitude, and follow it, through time and geography, it won't matter which line you take for they all go back to that bit of land in the wine dark sea and to the one who held out the skein of thread, as if love itself was made suddenly material.

UNDERTOW

The other night I was listening to Sibelius' second symphony. The news of the last days were full of what happened in Charlottesville. And not long ago another police shooting in Minneapolis, and the bombing of an Islamic center in nearby Bloomington. Much of the bad national news is local now. I was thinking about that, reading an article on tactics for stopping neo-Nazis, seeing all these images flash by on my computer screen. And Sibelius' music kept rolling, as if a rhythmic undertow kept all the forces moving across the aural landscape, one moment sounding like the forces of war on march and everything on its way to lurch over a cliff. And then there was a bright moment when a light begins to glow, and all that sound and fury fills with that light, and the terrible undertow transforms, it becomes itself a monumental vessel of light, and all things reveal their true nature, that we are light and of the light, and finally the light *will* prevail.

At Home in the Broken Vessel

I picture a gathering of a few souls,
perhaps over a cup of tea, and
they talk about their own vessels.

One says: My vessel fails at almost
everything he does. I don't think I have
seen anyone with a life of such failure,
in every area of his life. I'm not sure
he will ever have a lasting relationship.
The Soul spoke with brimming pride.

Another Soul spoke, also with intense pride:
My vessel made a great mistake.
Driving drunk one night
he accidentally killed a young woman
in a car crash. My vessel is in jail now.

The last Soul jumped in, with as much
boastful pride as the others:
My vessel is in a loveless marriage.
She is stuck in her life in every way
you can imagine. She is sad all the time
and I doubt she will ever choose
what is best for her.

The Souls nod at each other, knowing.

Then with great joy, each returns to
its own broken vessel,
going back to their perfect homes.

After the Gateway Opened

When I was a teenager I once composed music
to Emily Dickinson's "I felt a funeral in my brain."
Death was hammering black keys
as far down as my left hand could reach.
What did those repeating cannonball notes open?
My chest became a door and they marched through.
The gateway was not wide enough and they
called for carpenters who sawed at my sides
with knives and axes and the door widened and
as the dead filed by they left gifts:

> the emerald earring I always wear,
> salt shakers and an owl incense burner,
> a teapot from Japan, antique dessert plates,
> mixing bowls and baking pans,
> a floor lamp, a quilt, two woolen afghans,
> a mask of the goddess Kali, red tongue
> extruding from her black face,
> books and LP records,
> a notebook once belonging to my favorite
> high school English teacher filled with
> his taut curlicue handwriting,
> and the shelves heave with operas—
> so much Wagner—so many Ring cycles.
> Once a box arrived in the mail full of
> books and VCR tapes—
> I cannot throw them out because
> they are the only material things from my friend.

My home is the repository of the dead

and the flood of leavings only allow
space for a meditation cushion.

The other week a friend died in a car crash
and I locked the door.

My dead knock still.
I tell them I am done with the gifts.
They talk through the cracks of the molding,
day and night, begging to come through.
I am done with death.
Are there not other doors to walk through,
others who can bear the sweaty saws and heavy axes?
I am done with death.
Do you not hear their whispers?

Climbing the Golden Mountain

"...and silence is the golden mountain."
— *Jack Kerouac*

Listen. Turn
everything
off. When
the noise
of our lives
drifts away,
when the
chatter of
our minds
sinks into
that perfect
lake of
nothing,
then, oh
then we can
apprehend
that golden
mountain,
always there,
waiting for
us to be
still enough
to hear it.

Whimsy #1

After their inhabitants go to sleep, the houses share their dreams, the places they would visit if not tethered to the earth. One watched a program on Africa and wants to feel the rumble of Victoria Falls. Another would like to sit on top of Uluru in Australia. None of that says another, San Francisco is the place, where houses rub shoulders and dance up and down steep, city hills. In the darkest of night the houses whisper the story of one who did it. You can still see the empty foundations. One of them just picked up and left. No one knows where the house went. Not even a postcard. They hope the house found what it went searching for.

Time's Daydream

A group of people stand at
a train station where trains
no longer run.
Bored children grow restless,
not allowed to touch anything,
especially the benches
with toothy mouths.
The numbers on the station
clock run away and
the clock hands turn
into grasshoppers.
Someone asks in a loud voice,
"Is it now?"

FROM MAX ERNST'S "A WEEK OF KINDNESS, #8"

Pass me if you dare,
says the sentinel,
mostly man, head of a beast,
teeth made of glass,
sharp as moon rays that cut hearts
into diamond refuse
that litter ocean floors and feed
the unsated crabs.

Pass me if you dare!
the monster yells,
holding the lantern he stole from Eros,
burning with desire's last flame,
humanity's hope,
mankind's curse.
Do you not hear the tortured cries,
begging to snuff the flame forever?

Pass if you dare,
the wounded creature invites.
I am the guide through the empty
cellars, the eternal nights,
over the black seas,
past the fevered sighs of
angels and demons.
If you are afraid, you
are not afraid enough.

Pass me if you dare to live.

AT MERLIN'S REST

We sat at the table through the evening
conversations moving across
and around. In the corner musicians,
playing guitars, plunked melodies,
improvising songs, soon joined
by a concertina. We sat until
near closing, enjoying good food—
it was pie week!—drink, and
good company. If Heaven
is anything like this, it
might be a fine place for
an eternity.

THE OPPOSITE OF WAR

for Ardie Medina

> *"…the opposite of war is not so much peace as civilization"*
> – Michael Longley

The opposite of war is my neighborhood where baristas serve
coffee to tired and harried strangers with the dignity of sleek
waiters at the Saint Paul Hotel,

where a man plays the guitar with friends singing favorite Beatles
songs to all who will hear,

where a scholar sitting by himself deciphers lines of Homer as if all
the questions of the world will be answered by this vital work;

the opposite of war is a classroom where a high school teacher
makes sure that when the little girl from Sudan enters the
classroom, even if there is not a desk, she will get something to sit
on and something to write with,

a bus driver who rejoices that the next person entering the bus
does not yell at her,

a cook in a Middle Eastern deli whose first home was not
America and wonders how long he will be able to stay, far from a
world at war;

the opposite of war is a poetry reading where poets give voice to
their lives and hold humanity in the cups of their hands as if it is
precious and worth preserving.

In Praise

I praise next-door neighbors who cast opposing votes
and then go on living peacefully side by side.

      – Thomas R. Smith, "Politics" from *The Glory*

I praise the voters who believe in the mechanics of working governance.
I praise the peacemakers who never give up on the bold idea that we
      have better natures.
I praise all who see a human being first and not a label, and those,
      too, who seeing a label first then correct themselves.
I praise the gentle souls whose words often get left unsaid because
      others jump in.
I praise lovers of poetry who read from dog-eared books falling apart
      from so much reading.
I praise gardeners who believe flowers and all beauty must be nourished.
I praise the musicians who discover the true path to the soul.
I praise the silent ones who go their way unruffled.
I praise the wise ones who went before, their lanterns still guiding.
I praise the animal companions who so easily practice unconditional love.
I praise my family, I praise my friends—they know why.
I praise the strangers who show unexpected kindness.
I praise teachers who somehow find their inner patience most of the time.
I praise scholars who dive into history's deep end and sometimes
      come up for air.
I praise the animals seen and unseen who have their own desires.
I praise the books who held my hand in friendship when no one else
      would.
I praise the poets whose lives lovingly trace the path of the Word.
I praise the book makers and the booksellers who feed our souls.
And I praise each and every one of you, in whatever small way you
      choose life, and live against the grain.

I praise the artists, oh how I praise the artists, I will always praise the artists.

NOTES

"Reality Wears Us Thin": the first line comes from "Summer Meadow", Tomas Tranströmer.

"The Silver Skiff": The epigraph quotes "Descent and Defeat" by Georg Trakl.

The poem, "Whimsy #1" is inspired by a painting by my mom, Nora Moore, of the same name.

"Signs of the Times": Sources for poems in this section include

The Signs of the Times #2:

https://www.gaystarnews.com/article/vandals-break-lgbti-youth-center-rhode-island-hang-noose/

Signs of the Times #9:

http://www.kansascity.com/news/local/crime/article134581204.html

Signs of the Times #10:

http://www.startribune.com/shoving-match-erupts-inside-minneapolis-institute-of-art-one-involved-had-look-of-neo-nazi/414817964/

Signs of the Times #11:

http://www.jta.org/2017/03/01/news-opinion/united-states/muslim-veterans-offer-to-guard-jewish-sites-across-us

Signs of the Times #12:

https://www.thenation.com/article/lynching-university-maryland-campus/

Signs of the Times, #16:

http://www.ozaukeepress.com/content/valedictorian-dares-disturb-universe

ACKNOWLEDGMENTS

"A wolf dreams he is me," *The Talking Stick, 26*, 2017.

"At Home in the Broken Vessel, *The Talking Stick, 25*, 2016.

"Before the May Day Dance," Second Place, League of Minnesota Poets "Musica Award," 2018.

"Cosmic Molten Chocolate Souffle: a bricolage," Honorable Mention, League of Minnesota Poets "Florence Hynes Willette Memorial Award," 2018.

"Do not reject the world," *The Talking Stick, 27*, 2018.

"Ganymede with the Eagle," First Place, League of Minnesota Poets "Heartland Poets Award," 2018.

"If I was Human No More," *Martin Lake Poetry Workshop*, 2016.

"Lorca, the Moonlight, and Me," In Luczak, R. (Ed.), *Lovejets: Queer Male Poets on 200 Years of Walt Whitman*. Minneapolis, MN: Handtype Press, 2019.

"The Lost Language," *Saint Paul Almanac: On a Collected Path*, 11, 2017; reprinted in *Fierce Lament*, Gage, C. J., (Ed.), Red Bird Chapbooks, 2018.

"Manning Up in the 21st Century," *Water-Stone Review*, 20, 2017.

"Ode to Karen's Pulla," *Martin Lake Journal*, 2017.

"Reality Wears Us Thin," *Martin Lake Journal*, 2017.

"The Silver Skiff," *Poetry City* (Volume 8), 2018.

"Undertow," Honorable Mention, League of Minnesota Poets "Cracked Walnut Award," 2018.

"When Words Had Power," *Martin Lake Poetry Workshop*, 2016.

"Trace of Us," *Martin Lake Poetry Workshop*, 2016.

Michael Kiesow Moore is the author of the poetry collection, *What to Pray For* (Nodin Press). He was born in Cheyenne, Wyoming, and grew up in Florida and Maryland. He has made Minnesota his home for many years, now living in Saint Paul. His work has appeared in numerous journals including *Poetry City, Water~Stone Review, The James White Review,* and in anthologies such as *Queer Voices* (Minnesota Historical Society Press), *Lovejets: Queer Male Poets on 200 Years of Walt Whitman* (Squares & Rebels), and *Fierce Lament* (Red Bird Chapbooks). His honors include a Minnesota State Arts Board fellowship, a Loft Mentor Series Award, and an artist residency at Kalani Retreat Center in Hawai'i. He is active in Twin Cities literary arts, founding both the Birchbark Books Reading Series and the Loft Peace and Social Justice Writers Group, and serving on the board of directors at Cracked Walnut. He teaches creative writing classes in the Twin Cities at various locations including the Loft Literary Center.

He especially enjoys opportunities to collaborate with artists. His poetry hung on the walls at Banfill-Locke Arts Center in 2015 along with art by his mom, Nora Moore, and textile artist Karen Searle in the show titled "Textural Forms." His poetry was selected for recent Poet-Artist Collaborations at the Crossings in Zumbrota, Minnesota. He also collaborates with cellist Lars Ortiz for unique presentations of word and music. He can even be found dancing with the Ramsey's Braggarts Morris Men.

More information can be found on Michael's website, *www. michaelkiesowmoore.org.*